From the Secret Cave

By Brian Holley

3rd Edition

"An expression of wisdom, ancient and modern, to bring meaning to those of us who live among the chaos of the 21st century."

Cover pictures: Cappadocia, Central Turkey.

Copyright © 2012/2016/2019 Brian Holley
Individual poems may be used free of charge. Selling without prior written consent is prohibited. Obtain permission before redistributing. In all cases this notice must remain intact.

ISBN.13: 978-1-0985-9204-2

In the secret cave of the heart,
two are seated
by life's fountain. The separate ego
drinks of the sweet and bitter stuff,
Liking the sweet, disliking the bitter,
While the supreme Self drinks
sweet and bitter
Neither liking this nor disliking that.
The ego gropes in darkness, while the Self
Lives in light.
So declare the illumined sages
And the householders who worship
The sacred fire in the name of the Lord.

The Katha Upanishad
Translated by Eknath Easwaran

TABLE OF CONTENTS

Foreword	1
About the book	2
Notes on the third edition	5
The Sutras	6
My Sages (A list of sources)	136
About the author	139

Foreword

Words written on a page are congealed language. They have none of the breath that quickens the spoken word, neither do they carry the intonation of meaning that can only come from a living body; the reader must provide these, otherwise the book remains fruitless and dead.

To avoid this, a process must be gone through to convert the symbolic letters, punctuation and spaces back into living experience, and this may take years. That's why books such as these should never be read only once, but again and again until, once more, the language becomes living currents in the river of understanding.

Brian Holley
Weobley, Herefordshire
June 2019

About the book

What I've tried to encapsulate in the inadequate medium of words are not statements of fact, though sometimes that may appear to be the case. My 'openings', as Quakers call them, are expressions of an intuition that is felt rather than known. The style of the text is designed to speak to the heart rather than the head. That's why I've written them in poetic-prose and make use of metaphor, allegory and paradox. Only when the heart hears will readers need to use rational thought to express their own openings to others – if they really feel this to be appropriate, necessary or even possible.

If you don't agree with something or find a passage to be difficult or obtuse, I suggest you don't struggle with it. Let it rest in stillness on your mind. If it still doesn't make sense, move on. The sense may fall into place when you've read all the sutras. In a few years time I myself may not agree with some of the thoughts expressed here or I may want to express them differently. As scientist Jocelyn Burnell says in Quaker Faith and Practice, this is simply my working hypothesis.

I use four significant terms: **'The Way', 'The One', 'The Self' and 'The Enabling'.** The first three are terms widely used in English translations of ancient texts to refer to what may be thought of as 'the divine'. 'The Way' is a common translation of the Chinese word Tao. It is also a word Jesus used in reference to himself, and before they were labelled Christians, the early disciples called themselves 'Followers of the Way'.

'The One' and 'The Self' are common references to the divine in the Indian Vedic scriptures, especially the Upanishads. I added a fourth term, 'Enabling', which, in my view, expresses the way in which 'divinity' functions. The idea of an Enabler rather than a Creator, I believe, is novel and, for me, critical to my personal understanding of the nature of whatever it is we refer to as 'the divine'. It seems to me that evolution proceeds on the basis of what can be, not what some supernatural being decides will be (See sutras 13, 18, 24 & 30). This appears to indicate, not a process of intervention, which would require force, but an enabling that is totally without coercion. This idea agrees with Jesus's teaching in Matthew Chapter V (The Sermon on the

Mount) about a non-violent 'God'. The passage is more about the nature of the God that Jesus preached than it is about the way his followers should behave. This is clear from the last verse which says, "Therefore be perfect and your father in heaven is perfect."

This portrayal of a totally non-violent 'God' accords beautifully with the Tao of the Tao Te Ching. It is not in the nature of the Tao to force things, but to bring things to pass by enabling the energies that exist in nature to fulfil their role. The well-known Taoist term for this is 'wu wei', often translated 'non-ado'. Our role is simply to co-operate.

In mystical thought, the terms, 'The Way', 'The One', 'The Self' as well as my own 'Enabling' refer to what is variously described as: the 'Atman' or 'Self' of the Upanishads, the 'Christ within' which Paul referred to in Colossians Chapter VII, the 'Friend', used by the Sufi poet, Rumi, in reference to Allah, the 'Lover' of Kabir and, of course, the Tao and the Constant of the Tao Te Ching. My use of the terms has none of the overtones of the interventionist 'God' of Judaism, Christianity and Islam but may be interpreted as 'God' if you wish.

I also refer to **'The Self' and 'The True Self'** (traditionally expressed as proper nouns). This reference is used in contrast with 'the false self', which is invariably expressed in the lower case. The 'false self' is the individual self-awareness that develops out of the ego (expressed as the persona, a Latin word which represented the mask Roman actors spoke through). Our sense of self comes from experiences of internal and external influences. Internally we have our natural instincts and inherited predispositions which colour our memories of family, peer and cultural influences along with other experiences of life. Our sense of self is shaped largely from our understanding and feelings about the opinions those around us have of us. It's 'who you think you are', who you'd like to be' or perhaps 'who you'd like others to think you are,' but not who you truly are.

Much is blamed on the ego, some gurus speaking of the death of the ego. My view is that the ego's role is essential to providing a sense of self-identity and it does this by discernment and differentiation. However, that rôle can easily be perverted by prejudices and preferences arising from culture and predilections. The outcome is coloured by our fears and desires, and likes and dislikes. Therefore the individual self-identity that evolves is invariably a 'false self'. That doesn't mean it's a bad self, but simply that it's not a true self. Only in-as-much as we experience 'The True Self' do we see the 'false self' for what it is and are able to reduce its influence on our behaviour. (Sutra 154).

The old brain and the new brain (Sutra 160) are references to the limbic system and the cerebral cortex. The limbic system is part of the most primitive area of the brain also called the reptilian and mammalian brain. From it arise most of our base emotions: fear, anger, desire and sexual urges, etc. Our instincts, known as 'the four Fs', arise from here too: the instinct to fight, flee, feed or (ahem) mate. They are triggered by the five senses. The new brain, the cerebral cortex and frontal lobes, is the seat of reasoning, intuitive creativity and empathy.

A large part of human behaviour problems arise from having a primitive brain, evolved to meet the basic survival needs of a hunter-gatherer culture, in tandem with a more recent brain, evolved to be rational and creative. We have now reached a point when we can co-operate with nature in evolving our own consciousness. If we don't do that, the trajectory of our current path will lead to our self-destruction.

When I refer to **'Sages'** I mean those who recorded their wisdom, both in the distant past and recently. The term 'wise' refers largely to those who, having broken free of doctrinal constraints, continually seek and maintain a personal experience of the ineffable.

The word **'you'** is a reference to myself, not to other people. My journal is a collection of reminders to myself rather in the style of Marcus Aurelius's *Meditations*. However, when you come across a statement that addresses 'you', you might wish to imagine it's the 'you' that's talking to yourself about yourself.

In common usage the word **'realise'** means to understand or perceive. More often than not I use it in its original sense, 'to make real'. In psychological-speak, perhaps I could say 'actualise'.

The language I use is occasionally archaic, which is to reflect that the thoughts expressed are ageless, and their truth has withstood the ravages of time and human deviousness. You will find the ideas here expressed in many different scriptures and spiritual works. Although I quote from my sources extensively I have not shown the sources. There is only one ultimate source of wisdom and by not disclosing the sources that's what I infer.

Some 'opening's have several versions which may be amplification, simplification or just plain repetition. I wondered if I should edit these to create some sort of coherence, but decided it was better, in general, to let the work take its own course, in accordance with the principle of 'enabling'. After all, each journal entry was made in a different context and maybe that lends a nuance according to its place in the whole. Often a statement is not universally true and much is understated or left unsaid to allow readers to derive meaning from their own circumstances. The whole work is an expression of wisdom, ancient and modern, to bring meaning to those of us who live among the chaos of the 21st century. Little is original. These passages are simply the crumbs I've gathered "from under the table of the Sages" (Sutra17).

Notes on the third edition

In 2016/17 I reviewed 'From the Secret Cave' and realised that I have moved on quite a long way during the preceding four years. I therefore did some serious editing, replacing whole sutras and clipping off the ends of many, since I noticed I had a habit of wanting to hammer home things that had already been adequately said. Because I intend this to be a printed version I've also changed the order and numbering of some sutras to reduce the number of pages and be economical with our earth's resources.

. . . and, dear American friends, I've stuck to UK English spelling throughout.

One

You cannot see the One or touch it.
You cannot point to it or explain it.
It has all wisdom
But you cannot ask its advice.
It has all knowledge
But you cannot learn from it.
Though you can see where it has been,
You cannot see where it is going.
Yet when you experience it
You realise it.
When you realise it
You have found yourself.

Two

Knowledge of the Way is not higher knowledge.
Higher knowledge is always gain.
Knowledge of the Way is always loss.
It is the knowledge of the babe
Not the adult.
Not a knowledge to be learned,
But to be unforgotten.

You do not find it by climbing up,
But by sinking down.
It is to know as every child knows,
As every plant and every creature knows.

To know the Way,
Stop rationalising
And look within.

Three

There are those who follow the Way
Without knowing it.
They do what is natural to them
For the Way is not about words,
But action.

How much better than those
Who know the Way
And follow it only that they may be observed.

Most blessed are those
Who, in their actions,
Follow the Way consciously
For love.

Four

Words are only words.
Meaning is something else.
To confuse words with meaning
Is like thinking the flavour is in the food,
Instead of on your tongue.

Five

No two fires are the same.
Every flame is unique.
Yet everyone recognises what a flame is
And enjoys the heat.

The fire does not create
Its own light.
It is the light of the sun
Being given back.

The wise don't copy others.
Their wisdom arises
from the laying down of their lives.
They know that the light they have
Is not theirs.

Six

Both the mountain and the valley
Receive the same blessings from heaven,
Yet the mountain is bare
and the valley fertile and lush.

Neither the mountain nor the valley
Hold on to their gifts of grace.
They yield them up to that
From which they came.

The sun rises and sets
On the male and the female alike,
Yet it is the female who brings forth
the gift of the next generation.

Seven

There is much to be learned from scriptures,
And much to be forgotten.
Just as in evolution, the body sheds
That which no longer is fit to survive,
So regenerated minds shed that
which it is no longer fit to think.

Eight

You would not confuse the water
With the well from which it is drawn.
Yet they are not mutually exclusive.
The one gives expression to the other.
Believing doctrine
Is not experience of the Way.

The Way is not found in words.
It does not arise from the operation of the head
But from the operation of the heart.
Therefore its fruits are not words,
but love and compassion.

Nine

There is only one Being,
And it expresses itself in our being.
To be conscious of this
is to know the One.

Ten

Life has little to offer
Those who refuse to die,
But to die successfully,
One has to know how to live.

Eleven

To follow the Way
Is like dissecting an onion.
Much has to be discarded to find the heart.
And at the heart of the heart,
One finds nothing.

Twelve

Religion is a surrogate mother.
Her role is to bring her children to adulthood.
Her failure makes them cling to her
Long after they should have left home,
Or depart from her in bitterness and anger.

The wise seek not
That which is to be belonged to or believed
But the realisation of that
Which they already are.

Thirteen

The Enabling is like a mighty river.
 High in the mountain
Its source seems insignificant.
Fed by many tributaries,
It will cut a ravine – if it can.
It will spread out across a flood plain – if it can.
It will form a lake – if it can,
And, if it can, plunge down a fall.
But always it finds its way back to the ocean

The Sages were like mighty rivers.
They did not struggle against the Enabling
But allowed it to direct their paths.
They ever contemplated the return.

Fourteen

The lens of the ego
Has been ground by trouble.
The unenlightened see only what it allows.
The wise have put aside
Their warped lenses
And see all things anew.

Fifteen

Little is the space
within the skull.
When the mind is beset
By fear, regret and unrequited hope,
The space is further diminished.

The Way fills all the universe.
It cannot be diminished
by space or time.

Stand on a hill,
Let your consciousness soar
as the buzzard soars
And let the universe fill you.

Sixteen

Be frugal in keeping
And ruthless in discarding.
What was precious
In one generation,
May be dangerous
In the next.
We still treat with salicylic acid
But not with tortoise brain and honey.
We no longer bleed,
But transfuse.

Those who hold on
To that which should be let go
Look foolish among the wise
And are a threat
To those who are not.

Seventeen

In the One
The multitude of things
become manifest,
Yet it holds on to nothing
With a grasping hand.

The wise are happy in their poverty.
Though surrounded by plenty
They own nothing
So have nothing to lose.

All the wise hold dear
is a bag of crumbs
Gathered from under the tables of Sages.
It is the most precious thing they have.

Eighteen

The Way has no destination in mind.
Its path cannot be plotted.
It cannot be surveyed.
It does not force its route

With simplicity and patience
It finds a course,
Enabling to be what can be,
Though a million years in its becoming.

Thus the wise have no ends in mind
And need no force to achieve them.
They live in peace
Who are as the Way
From which all things arise.

Nineteen

To overcome the ego
Behold the Way.

To attend the ego's false self
is to look down.
To attend the Way
Is to look out.
To attend the ego's false self
Is to serve the ego.
To attend the Way
Is to make the false self servant
Rather than master.

Twenty

The aim of consciousness
Is not the aim of the body.
The body seeks survival,
Consciousness seeks transcendence.
That is why the mind must rule the body.
Not to do so
Is to let the body rule the mind;
The slave to rule the master.

Twenty One

That which is temporal is temporary.
Those who seek to become something
Are joined with the temporal
And forever are not.
In the temporal
There is no end to the search for meaning.
The One always is.
Those who seek to be
One with the One
Forever are.
When joined with the One
The search for meaning is meaningless.

Twenty Two

That which can be fathomed
 Is not the Way.
The wise do not try to fathom the Way,
They rest in its enabling.

Since the beginning
Knowledge has been known.
The wise don't claim
To have achieved knowledge.
They know that knowledge
Does not belong to them.
They belong to it.

Twenty Three

People mistakenly think
In getting the answer to "What?"
They have the answer to "Why?"
The wise know that the answer to "What?"
Is as endless as pi.
The answer to "Why?"
Is ever the same.

Twenty Four

Where the One can, it enables.
Where it can't enable, it protects.
When it can no longer protect, it trusts.
Where it can no longer trust, it hopes
When hope is done, it perseveres.
When perseverance does not succeed,
It never ceases to love.

Twenty Five

You ask for proof of the Enabling?
Sleep and awaken.
Breathe in, breathe out.
Eat and enjoy.
Jump in the air
And you will return to the ground.
Stop using force
And matters will settle
Of themselves.
Choose to live
By that which has always been within you.

Twenty Six

The transcendent is seen in the immanent.
If this were not so,
How could we know the Way?
Everything has its own voice,
To those who have ears to hear.
To the deaf
All things are temporal.
To poets
All things are temporal and symbolic.
To the wise
All things are immanent and transcendent.

Twenty Seven

Have without possessing.
Belong without being possessed.
Comprehend without knowing.
Be without becoming.
Care without fearfulness.
This is the way of the 'Enabling'.
What you see is what you get.
What you don't see
Is how you got it.

Twenty Eight

Some found a god with an ego
Like their own
But eventually became disgusted
With him.
The Sages went beyond
The pairs of opposites
Which guide the ego.

The 'Enabling' has "no desires for itself".
It does not demand to be heard,
Yet all those who know it hear it.
It does not demand to be loved
Yet all those who know it love it.
It does not demand to be obeyed.
Yet all those who know it obey it.
Some say that is the Enabling's vulnerability,
But the wise know it is its strength.

Twenty Nine

The wise do not label things as 'good' or 'bad',
They regard all things as 'right'.
Thus they are free from fear and desire.

The way of peace
Is the path to love.
The path to love
Is the way to joy.

Those who have found the Way
Are those who, without fear
Have looked within.

Thirty

The Way is nameless and unseen.
It is not cause but enabling.
It inhabits the spaces in between
And does not impose itself on that which is.
Yet in it all things consist.

The wise understand this as being
Like oil that lubricates the engine,
Not that which fuels the locomotion.
As the unseen it is unknown.
As the ever present it is known.

Thirty One

Facts are not truth.
Truth is not fact.
Facts are many.
Truth is one.
Therefore the wise seek not form
But the reality behind the form.
Fact stands lonely
In the multitude of its forms.
When wise people join meaning to fact,
Fact always points to the Way.
Where did the Sages find meaning?
They looked within.

Thirty Two

Nothing was made perfect
That perfection may be revealed.
Failure reveals success.
Doubt reveals faith.
Despair reveals hope.
Darkness reveals light.
Sorrow reveals joy.
The wise do not strive to be perfect.
They recognise perfection within themselves
And rest in it.
Only by choosing not to be perfect
Can you enter with joy
Into the sorrows of the world.

Thirty Three

When you cannot know,
You can only trust.
The Sages were those who
Stepped out of the boat,
Walked on insubstantial water
And received wisdom from the wind.
This is the path of love.
This is the way of the 'Enabling'.

Thirty Four

It is in the nature of Nature to nurture.
'The Enabling' does not discriminate.
Freely it nurtures all.
The wise choose
What is to be nurtured
And what to let die.
They return constantly
To the ground of their being.

Thirty Five

The One ever shines.
That is the nature of the One.
Thought is but shadow
Cast by clouds.
The wise let them pass
And wait patiently
For the return of the light.

Thirty Six

The sacred is not in the form.
The sacred is in the symbol.
The symbol is not in the form,
The symbol is in those
In whom meaning arises.
To confuse form with symbol
Is to walk in darkness.
To experience the symbol
Is to know the Way.
For this reason the Sages
Were not angered by sacrilege,
But filled with compassion.
In the sacrilegious
They saw only blind persons
Surrounded by light.

Thirty Seven

The wise do not study to fill their brains
But to awaken their hearts.
They know a fathomless well
Of sweetest water
And do not calculate its depth
Or assess its purity.
Neither do they want to know its history.
Their sole aim is to drink.
Rumi said,
"Do not talk of the orchard,
Eat the fruit."

Thirty Eight

The Way has no direction.
It is not a prepared path.
Therefore the Way cannot be discerned
By where it's heading,
Only by where it's been.
For this reason men say
There is no purpose or direction.
The wise know the Way
Does not force itself
Upon an unwilling nature.
It enables nature
To find its own path
Toward a goal only the Way knows.
The wise feel the Way forming itself
Beneath their feet.

Thirty Nine

To the Sages scriptures
Were like wells in a flooded land.
They did not allow their hearts
To be governed by the words of men.
They recognised sweet water
Wherever it could be found.
How did they do this?
By that which was within them.

Forty

The wise know
A place in the soul
Which has never been wounded.
Therefore, none can wound them.
Those who would wound,
Wound themselves.
To rail against the good
Is to rail against the good in yourself.
The more you rail
The less you can forgive yourself.

Forty One

What do you seek?
There is nothing there
That is not here,
Nearer than your breath.
Subtle as gossamer,
Fiercer than the sun,
Unceasingly it is the eternal source.
Do not seek it.
Realise it.

Forty Two

Fear is not compassion.
Compassion is not fear.
Those who are anxious for others
Are anxious for themselves.
Those who love
Know no fear.

Forty Three

The more you injure,
The more you are forgiven.
The more you injure,
The less you can forgive yourself.
Therefore, the wise know how to forgive,
They follow the Way
And injure no one.

Forty Four

Truth is not meaning.
Meaning is not truth.
Yet to the wise, the two become one.
Meaning is to be understood.
Truth is to be experienced.
Meaning may change.
Truth is One.
Fearful are those
Who have meaning without truth.

Forty Five

Violence is always wrong.
Though sometimes
it may become inevitable
It is always wrong.
It is the progeny of fear,
And a violation.
People fear because they see
only the temporal.
They deal only
with the temporary.
For this reason they become violent.
The wise see all things as themselves
And deal only with the One.
For this reason they are at peace
And bring peace to all their dealings.

Forty Six

Showers of rain
Come in their season
And leave all things refreshed.
Yet you cannot tell when they will come
or from where.
The Sages were wonderful lovers
Because they knew how to surrender to love.
Yet they knew that ecstasy
isn't something to hold on to.
It passes like spring showers
Leaving all life refreshed.

Forty Seven

Fools walk backwards into the future
Thinking that the past
Is leading them somewhere.
The wise leave the past behind.
In the eternal now
They step into the abyss
Knowing that the Way
Will form beneath their feet.

Forty Eight

In The Enabling all things consist.
The wise know this.
For them good and evil flow together,
Success and failure do their work.
Never do the wise say,
"This should not be happening to me."
Thus, having nothing to fear,
They experience no calamities,
But know how to rest in the One.
Yet in this knowledge
The wise are not complacent.
They look upon the sufferings of others
And weep.
They see others suffering
And act.
When asked, they lend.
When begged from, they give.
This is the way of the One.

Forty Nine

Consciousness is the light of the mind.
Shine it on what you will
And the mind will be filled with it.
Light up fear
And you will be fearful.
Light up desire
And you will be lustful.
Light up hate
And you will be hateful.
The wise know how to control
the light of consciousness.
Light up peace
And you will be peaceful.
Light up love
And you will be loving.
Light up joy
And you will be joyful.
It is a simple thing
To change your mind.

Fifty

To be at peace
Is not to be inactive
But to act peacefully.
The Sages acted constantly
Without becoming tired.
They knew how to be enabled
By that which they found within themselves,
As well as that which was without.
Thus, in the time it takes
To perform one task,
The Sages performed a multitude
And still had energy for more.
This is the way of the One.

Fifty One

Not to understand that you are enabled,
Not to understand the Way,
Not to be in relationship with the One,
Is de-meaning.

Fifty Two

Transcendence is not a reward.
It is your natural state.
Self-denial is not a method.
It is a reward.
To deny yourself
And not to experience transcendence
Is a calamity.
They have the wrong expectation
Who deny themselves
In order to gain.
Therefore the wise do not deny themselves
They transcend the ego
Knowing that desire will fall away.

Fifty Three

The wise recognise that the air they breath
Does not belong to them;
The light that lightens them
Is not theirs;
The water of which their bodies are composed
Did not originate with them,
And they depend on the sacrifice of death
For every morsel of food.
If they do not own their bodies,
What do they own?

Fifty Four

You cannot strengthen that which is strong.
You cannot perfect that which is perfect,
You cannot make wise that which is wise.
Therefore the Sages diminished themselves daily
So that the Way could be made plain.

Fifty Five

Only the ego takes offence.
The wise are not 'nice' to people,
When people need them to be honest.
They are not afraid of offending
With plain speech,
Neither are they offended
By the offence others take.
Untruth takes many forms.
Truth is ever the same.

Fifty Six

If the One intervened,
It would not be the One.
If the Way took action,
It would not be the Way.
Enabling takes place
Out of the nature of things.
Nothing is good.
Nothing is bad.
Everything is right.
Therefore the wise are untroubled
By questions of good and evil.
Yet they know how to avoid evil
And follow good.
How do they know this?
By that which is within them.

Fifty Seven

Love without detachment is attachment.
Detachment without love is indifference.
Those who follow detachment alone
Cannot know joy.
Those who follow love alone
Will be beguiled.
The who know love with detachment
By detachment are freed from the bonds of desire and fear,
And by love are ever sure footed on the path.

Fifty Eight

When people said
The Way is ours,
The Sages smiled
And travelled on.
When people said,
The Way is yet to be,
The Sages smiled
And sat at ease.
When the Sages said
The Way is here within,
The people mocked
And asked for proof.
The proof is ever present,
Available to all whose minds are free
From the contradictions of doctrine
And the tether of opinion.

Fifty Nine

The promptings of the Enabling
Is like the ticking of a clock,
Which the wise wind,
Morning and Night.
They use the key of self-purification,
Which leads to peace;
The experience of peace,
Which leads to love;
The experience of love,
Which leads to joy;
What is the point
Of an ever-present clock
That is never heard?

Sixty

Who will deflect the Enabling from its path?
Can you make the One, variable?
Can you stop the Way from being the Way?
A Sage said,
"Love will always trust,
Always hope,
Always protect,
Always persevere."
When the wise discover this
They put away their garments of office,
Stop reciting their prayer requests,
Cease their rituals,
And disperse the crowds.
They seek only to be at one
With the Enabling.

Sixty One

The fruits of the Enabling
Are peace, love and joy.
Yet it does not itself experience these fruits.
These are gifts of grace.
The wise experience them
In knowing the Way
and living close to the One.

Sixty Two

A Sage said:
That which is not experienced positively,
Must be experienced negatively.
Project your fear on others
And you will hate them.
Project your desires on others,
And you will blame them.
To think yourself sane
And everyone else mad,
Is the first sign of insanity.
The wise understand
the workings of the mind.
They know from whence the instincts arise
And understand their motives.
Thus they are able to turn their energies
To their own advantage
And avoid calamity.
The wise do not give up things
In order to gain merit.
They let things go
That are a hindrance
To the Enabling.

Sixty Three

What do you see?
Twenty two people
Kicking inflated leather
Around a field?
You see dedication, training and skill.
You see commitment, self-sacrifice and relationship.
You see empathy, compassion and the joy of success.
What you see
Is not what you get.
What you get
Is already deep within you.
While others enjoy
Their day out at the match,
The wise are doubly joyful.
They perceive the depths
from which joy arises.

Sixty Four

The Way is like the wind.
No one knows from where it comes,
Or to where it goes.
Hence the wise do not plot a course.
With open hearts
They hear the master's voice
In the mouths of strangers,
In a fiery bush,
In the words of a book,
In a radio play,
And the song of a shepherd.
To them it is unmistakable,
Even when, what they hear,
Turns their world upside down.

Sixty Five

The wise have no private ends to serve.
They do not use others
For their own purposes.
This they learned from the One.
Though it is endless in its giving,
The One takes nothing.
Because it is the servant of all,
All things are its servant.
The wise give
Without counting the cost.
They know that it is in giving
That they receive.

Sixty Six

The reason the Sages strove
Toward an ever higher place
Was not for their own salvation.
They realised they could not help another
Reach higher than they already stood.
That is why the One is above
As well as below;
Is transcendent
As well as closer than your breath.

Sixty Seven

Religion may fetter the ego's false self,
But it may fetter the True Self also.
It is natural to assume that words reveal the Way.
But they can equally conceal it.
At best words withdraw the veil,
unblock the wells,
roll back the stone from the tomb
To let the prisoner free.
A Sage said:
"It is not speech we should want to know.
We should want to know the speaker."

Sixty Eight

First discover who you are.
Failure in this leads to inventions of self.
Not to awaken to reality is a disaster.
It is to spend a whole life
Wondering what might have been.
The wise awaken
And discover the True Self.
They spend their latter years
learning how to live it.

Sixty Nine

Peace is not the absence of war,
It is the fulfilment of being.
That is why the wise seek peace.
It is their obligation to themselves
And to others.
Without peace love cannot flourish.
Without love, there is no joy.
Each is the fruit of the other.
All is the fruit of the One.

Seventy

To speak of 'my' and 'mine'
Is to separate oneself from the One.
You can only own
That which is not you.
The wise see "all things in themselves
And themselves in all things."
In spirit they are like beggars
Though everything is theirs.
For this reason they are without fear.

Seventy One

You cannot embrace another
With a stick in your hand.
Love cannot be driven in,
It can only be drawn out.
Love calls to love.
From the depths love responds.
Roll away the stone
And let love arise.

Seventy Two

They have to speak bravely
Who live in fear.
When all authority is outside you
What right have you to live?
The wise find authority within themselves.
This is why they walk fearlessly
Among the fearful.
Who is the authority of which we speak?
Who knows but the wise?

Seventy Three

There is a time to listen
To the mood of the body;
Its constraints, its demands.
There is a time to listen and obey.
There is a time to ignore
The mood of the body;
Its fears, its desires.
There is a time to dig deeper
And to persevere.
Not to know this
Is to be dragged about
By wild horses.

Seventy Four

There is the transcendent
And there is the immanent.
The wise recognise these two are the same.
Not to do so
Would be to live in separation.
In contemplation
The wise become one with the One.
In prayer the One becomes one with the wise.

Seventy Five

To hate the hater
Is to become entangled in hatred.
The wise look through the hatred
And see the One.
Thus their anger abates
And their compassion arises.
It is difficult to hate
One who loves,
   - But not impossible.

Seventy Six

No point in telling the unconscious
They are unconscious!
Better to tend their wounds
So they may awaken
When the time is right.
Unconsciousness is nature's unaesthetic.
To awaken them too early
Could inflict unutterable suffering.
Let them be, until they can bear the light.

Seventy Seven

There is the sound of a word
And the object of its reference.
Then there is the association of the two
Which is knowledge.
Is knowledge the word,
Or its referent
Or the association of the two?
Knowledge rests, not in the word,
 Not in the object of its reference,
 But in the mind of the wise.

Seventy Eight

You should always love an enemy,
Even the one who besets you
From within your own mind.
To fear an enemy
Is to feed one negativity
With another.
It is to lose the battle
Before it has begun.
To love an enemy
Is to disarm it
Before it can inflict harm.
When desires or fears arise,
Embrace them as dear friends.
Greet them with love,
Then bid them fond farewell.
Their power will dissipate.

Seventy Nine

To seek peace
For the sake of peacefulness
Is to find only placidity.
The surface of the lake
Is only calm
While there is no wind.
When the wind blows
The placid surface
 Shatters into a million pieces.
 But deep below the surface,
Stillness remains.
The wise know how to stay
In the dwelling place of the One.
Where peace reigns
The whole body is resonant with it.

Eighty

Toleration is the measure of maximum stress
An object can endure.
Therefore the wise are not tolerant,
They are accepting,
Not of opinions
But of those who hold them.
The wise know that they cannot know,
And that to think otherwise is folly.
Therefore they do not persuade
By clever argument,
Or undermine the opinions of others.
They live their lives
And let their living speak the truth.

Eighty One

No one struggles to die.
Unless they seek suicide,
They struggle to live.
But when the time comes
Dying is a simple thing.
You surrender to it.
The wise know how to die.
That is why they know how to live.
They know how to enter the tomb;
How to remain there for three days;
How to roll away the stone,
And how to walk out into new life.

Eighty Two

As the iris of the eye enlarges
When the lover beholds the beloved
So consciousness expands
In the presence of the One.
As lovers know only the moment,
So the One is only known
In the ever present Now.
Each moment,
Pregnant with possibilities,
Brings to birth what it can.
The wise only embrace the past
In order to lay it gently to rest.

Eighty Three

The foundations are laid
And the building grows.
Rooms are furnished
And the guests arrive.
They admire the building
And commend its owner
But who looks at the foundations
Upon which the whole structure stands?
The wise know that
Nothing can be seen
Without that which is unseen.
Nothing can stand
Without that upon which it stands.
Therefore they never forget
To spend time in the basement
Getting to know where their reality lies.

Eight Four

The little self prattles and plays,
Delighting in this and that,
While the One looks on
As lovingly as a mother.
All unknowing
The little self always gives expression
To the One.
The wise are the wise
Only because they are awake
To the source of their Enabling.

Eighty Five

The Sages say:
Fear and Desire,
Like two horses,
Pull the chariot of the body.
One horse pulls to the left,
The other to the right.
Only those who have firm control
Through the reins of the mind,
Can steer a straight course.
The wise are lords of their chariots.
The One is their charioteer.
Surrendering to the wisdom of the Enabling
Avoids calamity and loss.

Eighty Six

Tender as gossamer
Gentle as a breeze
Is the Enabling.
It does not create,
But its yearning brings into being
All that is.
Those who have ears to hear
Recognise its promptings
And live in peace.
Those who sleep
Both at night and at day
Know only the chaos of dreams.

Eighty Seven

The mind is the servant of the heart.
It's role is to fetch and carry.
Sad are those
Who are ruled by their minds.
For a servant makes a cruel master.
As one who has lived
At the beck and call of others,
It demands constant attention.
Woe betide those
Who do not jump to its every demand.
Yet when the mind knows its role
Peace fills the house.
For the heart is patient,
The heart is kind.
It does not envy,
It does not boast,
It is not self-seeking
And it keeps no record of wrong.
All things are enabled through the heart.
It is the dwelling place of the One.

Eighty Eight

You put your clothes in the laundry
And collect them in due time.
The clothes you put in
Are the clothes you get out,
But different.
Your clothing is fresh and neat.
So it is in the spiritual life.
What you put in,
Is what you get out,
The difference is,
Your experience.
To the wise,
All things are constantly renewed.

Eighty Nine

Be grateful for consciousness.
Be grateful for being aware of consciousness.
Be grateful for the gift of choice
Which arises from the awareness of consciousness.

Ninety

If you don't know what you want,
You'll settle for what you can get.
What will you settle for?
Intermittent chaos,
Or the ground of peace?
Conditional love
Or unconditional love,
The ground of your being?
The mediocrity of fickle happiness,
Or the ground of Joy?

Ninety One

To surrender to an enemy
Is to suffer defeat.
To surrender to the beloved
Is a victory.
As you surrender
So does the beloved.
It is the lowering of the barriers
To let love fill
The spaces between.
Thus, that which has been
From the beginning
Is realised.

Ninety Two

The Enabling does not impose things
As if it had a will.
It is not a creator
Who, like a clock maker,
Plans, brings things into existence,
Then maintains it and repairs it.

It is a longing
In the heart of the cosmos,
Alluring that which can be
To be.
The wise know that they do not produce the Way,
The Way produces them.

Ninety Three

The One calls for
no creed to honour,
No doctrine to subscribe to,
No ritual to follow,
Only the recognition of your own thirst,
And an openness
To receive fulfilment
Through simple wonder.
Let the silent springs arise
And flood the heart.

Ninety Four

Stop rearranging the furniture!
Be still in the beauty of your own soul
And the furniture will rearrange itself.

All that is demanded of a channel
Is that it is kept open.
Then the flood can reach the plain.
To be an enabler,
You have to allow the Enabling
To enable.

Ninety Five

Without diversity of form,
How can you understand being?
Mistaking form for being
Is the perennial error.
The wise perceive
That form is a memory
of both Truth and Error.
They know how to experience
Truth untrammeled.
They realise that the organising dynamic
Of their thoughts,
Is the organising dynamic
Of the Universe.

Ninety Six

The One is a vast emptiness
Ever replenished with good things.
What is more important
The container or the content?
Without the container,
Where would the content be?
The content continually changes,
Whereas the container
Remains ever the same.
The content is continually consumed,
Whereas the container
Is ever replenished.
Only the container knows
How to replenish itself.
Those who know how to eat from it,
Are satisfied only as those
Who encountered the Holy Grail.

Ninety Seven

Those who would be counted among the wise
Must become as little children.
They must learn what actions to take
And when to take them;
What words to say,
And when to say them.
They have to know how to remain
Close to the One
And to be parented
By the Enabling.

Ninety Eight

The Way is never mistaken
About its path
Or its destination.
Travelling apart from it
You arrive where you should not be.
Travelling with it is hard to do.
It takes, not the easiest route,
But the simplest.
Shortcuts are always dangerous;
Full of unexpected hazards.
The discipline of the Way
Is to get to where it takes you
Without thought of where you want to be.

Ninety Nine

The artist, writer, poet and priest
Have access to the unseen
Through imaginative discernment.
It is their role to inspire.
If they fail in this,
They are no better than
Drawers, draughters and administrators.
The world has more than enough of these.

One Hundred

When a loved one dies
For what do you weep?
A decrepit body
Or the milieu of the One?
Yet the One is
Not something you can lose,
Like a friend.
So what is the loss you mourn?
You have lost a unique expression
Of the Enabling
That manifested itself
But once
In one who is no more.
Weep now.
For never again
Will there be such a manifestation
Of the ineffable.

One Hundred and One

The young face diminishment with hope.
For this reason
They never come to terms with it.

The middle-aged have learned
To accept diminishment
As part of life.
For this reason
They rarely come to terms with it.

Old age is a diminishment
Without hope.
To accept it without fear
So that it is recognised
As a receiving back into joy
Takes a lifetime to learn.

Best to make an early start.

One Hundred and Two

The learned understand
The principles of evolution
On many levels:
The universe,
The cosmos,
The planet,
Species,
And Societies.
The wise recognise
The operation of Enabling
Within themselves.
For this reason
They perceive the origin
Of tumult in themselves.
And are not overcome
By inheritance from ancestors.
They perceive the source
Of the tumult in others,
And have no fear.

One Hundred and Three

To be concerned with what you do,
And the way you are doing it,
Is to miss the whole point.
Even your motives
Are of no matter.
They may simply be
The excuses you make up for yourself.
Keep your mind on what you are
And all will make sense.

One Hundred and Four

The ancients recognised
That imagination is a dangerous thing.
For this reason
They populated their myths
With monsters and magic,
Whirlpools and witches,
Perverse Gods and deceptive serpents.
Who could believe such fabulous stories?

Had they an inkling
Of the reality of things,
As we do,
A "hand's breadth of certainty"
In an uncertain world,
Where would the richness of their wisdom be now?

One Hundred and Five

In each person
All meaning is embodied.
Yet to most
This is unknown.

The wise know how to express meaning
So that what seems meaningless
Becomes meaningful.

One Hundred and Six

Death is always experienced
By the bereaved
As something spiritual.
No matter what their beliefs
Or lack of them,
They feel that something
Is different.
In every marriage,
In every friendship,
There are three entities:
The lover, the beloved
And the loving.
When any one of these
Is missing,
The bond is broken
Which is why we grieve.

One Hundred and Seven

Those who think the scriptures
Tell them how to understand the One
Are mistaken.
To know about the One,
It is necessary experience the One.
Only then will the scriptures make sense.
As the Sage says,
"To the wise Scriptures are like wells
In a flooded land."

One Hundred and Eight

A Sage said:
"Words are the greatest enemies of reality."
But they can be emissaries of truth.
Your being is not defined
By the volume of sounds
That come from your mouth,
But by the quality of love
That comes from your heart.
The wise take care of the meaning
And the words take care of themselves.

One Hundred and Nine

When you know a thing to be
Sincere, trustworthy and beautiful,
Do you need to analyse it?
Understanding is important
Only in as much as that understanding
makes you sincere, trustworthy and beautiful.
That is known as the quality of understanding.

One Hundred and Ten

If you stay open enough
And quiet enough
For long enough,
Something wonderful will happen.

One Hundred and Eleven

Can you train a serpent
To do your will
As you can a cat or dog?
A snake charmer
May charm his charges
With Music,
But after the performance,
He keeps them in his basket.
The serpent is relatively harmless
As long as it is kept cool.
Therefore, keep cool
That which is reptilian within you.

One Hundred and Twelve

Truth does not expose herself
To the searing searchlight of the midday sun.
Beside still waters
She hides beneath the shade of trees.
She is yet more at home
In the cavern of the heart
Where candlelight and shadow
Animates the darkness.

One Hundred and Thirteen

Do you think you can offend the One?
Do you think that anything you do
Can alter the path of the Enabling?
Do you think that the Way
Will cease to be the Way
Without your effort
And that of those who
gather with you?
So why do you act
To defend the One
As if the One needed defending?
Why do you busy yourself implementing
This programme and that?
Why do you feel the need to explain
Instead of living the Way?
Is it the One you experience
Or a figment of your imagination?

One Hundred and Fourteen

If love is only
A heightened experience of emotion,
When the emotion is spent,
So is the love.
There is nothing wrong
With emotion
But the wise understand love
As a heightened experience
of acceptance.
Therefore their relationships
Will never become conflicted.
"Those who see all things
In themselves,
And themselves in all things
Have no fear."

One Hundred and Fifteen

Do you see life
As an obstacle course
Filled with fences and ditches,
Tunnels and walls?
To the One
These are pin pricks, gnat bites
And stones in the shoe.
Do you think the One
Will abandon you to your
Self-inflicted fate?
Its promptings come
Gentle as a summer breeze.
Noticing them
Puts everything in perspective.

One Hundred and Sixteen

Why value the rare
When it is the ubiquitous
That is most useful?
Can cows live on orchids?
Can humans thrive on gold?
The people honour leaders
Because of their unusual talents.
But it is the leaders
Who should honour the people
For without them
Where would they be?

Let the people respect leaders
But only inasmuch as they respect themselves.

One Hundred and Seventeen

Before you can speak
You must hear.
Before you can know
You must experience.
To know is not to understand.
To understand is not to know.
To understand
Is to imagine you have mastery.
Those who think they have mastery
Understand nothing.
Those who have experienced
The mystery of the One
Know the mastery of the One.

One Hundred and Eighteen

Words cannot bring to light
The light.
How can words
Reveal the ineffable?
Better are they
At exposing that which
Obscures the light.
Layer by layer
The skins of the heart: Desire, fear, pride, self-seeking,
Are revealed
So that the eyes may be opened
To see the perfection
That has always existed
Hidden in the heart.

One Hundred and Nineteen

Within the wood
Only the carver sees
An object of great beauty.
The task, the challenge,
Is to remove
All that conceals it.
The wise
Are uncarved blocks
Patiently waiting the removal
Of extraneous material.
The old one's hope rises
As the final dissolution approaches
As form returns to reality.

One Hundred and Twenty

Objects of desire
Are not the problem.

The wise have learned
To disengage from desire.
Therefore an object
Is only an object.
They can take it
Or leave it
Without damaging
Their integrity.

One Hundred and Twenty One

The social order
Is not something to be adhered to
Or rebelled against.
It is something that has to be
Transcended.
The wise know themselves
To be in the world,
But not of the world.
They see the world as it is
And judge it not.
They "suffer joyfully
The sorrows of mankind."

One Hundred and Twenty Two

No religious practice,
No scripture,
No meditation,
No mantra,
Is the path to happiness.
These are tools
Of demolition.
They clear the entrance
To the way to within.

One Hundred and Twenty Three

There is an ancient knowing
Beyond words:
A look, a sigh,
A frown,
A gentle touch.

Words contaminate truth.
They bend and twist it
Like a withy cane,
Being woven into a fence
With which to coral animals.

The knowing of the wise
Arises out of silence
And is born upon the wind.

One Hundred and Twenty Four

A Sage said that
The "tissue of your belonging"
Is tender.
Expose it to the harsh light
Of "analysis and accountability"
And it will become "parched
And barren."

Dwell always in the gentle light
Of the One,
Which dapples the cool shade
Beside pure pools
At the centre of your being.

One Hundred and Twenty Five

Do not imagine
That your imaginings are real.
The real you
Is not the one
That feels good, feels bad,
Feels indifferent,
But the one who observes
How you feel.
Reality begins
The moment you stop thinking about it.

What you say
Is wholly personal.
You express that which is within.
If others agree
Their agreement is wholly personal.
They agree, not with you,
But with the truth within themselves.
Do you want to share your reality?
Then love.

One Hundred and Twenty Six

How can the finite
Contain the infinite?
How can the temporal
Contain the eternal?
How can the corporeal
Contain the incorporeal
From which it came?
The unwise see all things in a mirror.
The wise see things as they are.

One Hundred and Twenty Seven

What exists
Is what can be.
What will exist,
Will be what can become.

The One does not set timetables.
There is no plan.
Only a simple longing
And an Enabling Love.

The wise surrender themselves
To a way that is not a way.
They step into the void
And the path forms itself
beneath their feet.

One Hundred and Twenty Eight

Too much sweetness
Makes you greedy.
Excessive sweetness
Makes you sick.
Rumi asks
"Do you want the sweetness
Of the food,
Or the Sweetness of the One
Who put the sweetness
In the food?"
You can have one or the other.
Not both at the same time.
Where your consciousness is
There is your experience.

One Hundred and Twenty Nine

The ego is the womb of the false self.
Fed by feelings and memories
The false self thrives
under the shadow of words
And the upsurge of feelings.
Thus it has
The appearance of existence.

It is a cuckoo
In a song bird's nest.
Dispossessed, the owner
Has become enslaved
To its constant demands.

The True Self looks on,
Alluring reality and form
Into congruency.

One Hundred and Thirty

Who has the patience to wait
Until words, thoughts, attitudes
Settle into sediment,
Revealing the still water of the mind?
Thus can others
See themselves reflected clearly
And all things are nourished
Without effort.

One Hundred and Thirty One

Feeling bad is just feeling.
Get beyond feeling bad.
Feeling good is just feeling.
Get beyond feeling good.
Beyond is one step away
Yet it takes you
To the end of the galaxy.

One Hundred and Thirty Two

A Sage said:
"All sorrow and all joy
Come from love."
Sorrow from its absence,
Joy from its presence.

One Hundred and Thirty Three

The ego-mind protects itself
By diminishing awareness,
Creating blind-spots
And changing what it remembers
To what it would prefer.

Diminished awareness
Leads to deception.
The more we lie
The deeper we bury
The True Self.

One Hundred and Thirty Four

Enlightenment is easy.
It is your natural state.
To find it, cease doing
And let everything fall away.

It arises not from wisdom
Or understanding.
They merely clear the obstructions
And the hindrances.

Enlightenment comes not
From building up,
But from breaking down.

Although enlightenment is easy
Maintaining it is difficult.
The body and mind
Constantly demand the
Attention of consciousness.
What your consciousness holds
Is one with you
For as long as you
Are conscious of it.

It is not what you do
That is important,
But the consciousness
In which you do it.
To stay enlightened,
Stay conscious.

One Hundred and Thirty Five

Beware of spiritual practices.
That which works for one
May not work for another.

Never judge a practice
By your own experience of it.
Some practices arise
Out of the intellect,
Some out of ego.
They have little to do
With the soul.
It is not difficult
To tell the difference.

One Hundred and Thirty Six

Be free
To question the reliability
Of all scriptures
And all teaching.
But never question
The integrity of the teacher
Whose heart is pure.
Though you disagree
With their theology, cosmology and eschatology,
Recognise a true heart.
Then sit at the feet of Masters
And let meaning arise.

One Hundred and Thirty Seven

To meet violence with violence
Gives meaning and justification
To violence, not to the cause.
A true cause
Needs no justification.
Its meaning is plain to all.
To meet violence with love
Renders violence meaningless.

One Hundred and Thirty Eight

Ignorance is not a hindrance
To the Enabling.
Wilfulness is.

In the face of ignorance,
It is amazing what the Enabling
Can accomplish.

To deliberately act
In full consciousness
Of that which hinders
Is not ignorance
But rebellion.

A Sage once said:
"Life is not about fulfilment.
It is about sacrifice."

One Hundred and Thirty Nine

Religion is a mother
Who must nurture her children.
She cleans them up
When they puke
And keeps them on a tight rein
Lest they stray
Into someone else's garden.

Her aim is
To bring them to adulthood
So they can live
Without her.
Yet in this
She often fails.
Thus her children
Remain children.
Obedient though they are
They resent her strictures
And long for freedom.
But she taught them
Fear of freedom
That they may support her
In the frailty of her age.

One Hundred and Forty

Consciousness is the spotlight
 Of the mind.
When a spotlight shines
On the ego,
Its false self takes centre stage
And performs,
Enjoying the adulation.
When a spotlight shines
On the True Self
Nothing can be seen.
How can light
Lighten light?

One Hundred and Forty One

Like all natural things
The body knows
How to be at ease
Within itself.
Left alone,
It is at one with the One.

The mind, so full of distraction,
Has to learn
To be at ease
Within itself.
Left alone,
It is at one with the ego.

Let not the mind disturb
The body at ease.
As lifelong friends,
Let them be at ease together.

One Hundred and Forty Two

Where were you
When your life's foundations
Were laid?
The one who builds the house
Is the rightful owner.
Acknowledge the owner
And understand yourself
To be a well loved guest.
But do not treat the house
As a place to which you come
And from which you go
At your will.
A place you visit as a holiday
From your normal residence,
Or retreat to in time of fear.
The owner longs for you to realize
You are as permanent a resident
As the One is.

A Sage said that
Everything of value
Comes from somewhere
Other than yourself.
Not as a gift, it comes,
But as a loan
Which must be ceaselessly renewed.

One Hundred and Forty Three

What is the point of beauty
That only titillates the eye
And sets the mind ablaze?
 The passion will fade
And the beauty with it.

That which is truly beautiful
Speaks neither to the eye
Nor to the mind alone,
But speaks truth
To the heart.

A Sage said:
"We see things, not as they are,
But as we are."

One Hundred and Forty Four

Challenge the ego
And it will take up arms.
Challenge the One
And it cannot be found.
Is it scared?
Has it fled?
Does it hide?

The ego is nothing,
But it thinks it is something.
That's why it takes up arms:
To conceal the fact
Of its non-existence.

The One is everything
But nothing of it can be found.
What is there to defend?

One Hundred and Forty Five

You cannot learn to swim
By reading a book,
Lying on your stomach
And waving your arms about.
Better to get into the pool.

Speech describes experience.
Experience transcends speech.
Hence it is said,
"Those who say they know, know not.
Those who know not, know."

Only those who know the One
Can speak of the One.
Only those who know the One
Understand what they say.

One Hundred and Forty Six

The Enabling
Does not protect life.
It protects the balance of life.

That which enables the atmosphere
Enables my breathing.
That which enables the water to flow
Enables me to drink it.
That which enables food to grow,
Enables me to eat it.

Life arises
Out of many dyings.
Thus the wise
Surrender themselves to the Enabling
Grateful for life
Grateful for death.

One Hundred and Forty Seven

In having everything
We have nothing.
Only in seeing the One
In everything
Do we have anything at all.
Then, though our possessions be few
We have everything we need.

Let us be grateful for the body
With which we feel the One.
Be grateful for the mind
With which we choose the One.
Be grateful for that within us
Which is the mysterious resting place
Of the One.

One Hundred and Forty Eight

Fools use words
To explain mystery
So that it is no longer mystery.
To the wise
All is mystery.
That is why they remain silent.

One Hundred and Forty Nine

To see the One
In another person,
We must lose sight
Of the other person.
As the Sage said:
"It is not speech which we should want to know:
We should know the speaker.
It is not mind we should want to know:
We should want to know the thinker."

One Hundred and Fifty

There is the journey
And the shadow journey.
Both head in the same direction.
The journey,
Experienced consciously,
Is full of joy.
The shadow journey,
Experienced unconsciously,
Is full of pain.
On the lighted path
Even pain is tinged with joy.
In the darkness
Joy is unknown.
"Walk in the light"
And though you walk
"Through the valley of the shadow of death,
You will fear no evil."

One Hundred and Fifty One

The ego discriminates and divides.
That is its role.
The One draws things into wholeness.
What else could it do?

The ego fusses about,
Evaluating and differentiating.

The One never fusses
And all things come together
Spontaneously.

One Hundred and Fifty Two

Material possessions
are neither good nor bad.
Attachment to them
Is a hindrance.
Disdain of them
Is a hindrance.

Attachment makes one feel superior.
Disdain makes one feel superior.
But superior to what?

The wise treat all things alike.
That is why they are rarely
Elated or cast down.

One Hundred and Fifty Three

Those who do not examine their beliefs
Deserve to be surprised.
Therefore welcome honest doubt
As an honoured guest.

You cannot find meaning
In the mouths of others.
The words of others
Can only cause
Your own meaning
To surface.

The wise do not follow blindly.
They are not led,
They are inspired.
Their path is not another's path
But their own.
Only the One
Has power over them
Which is why they are known
As those who walk alone.

One Hundred and Fifty Four

Long ago
People decided
How people should behave.
They named such behaviour culture.

Unencultured babies
Know what makes them happy and sad.
This is the beginning of ego's false self'.

Encultured children
Understand what should make them happy and sad
This is the maturing of ego's false self'.

Encultured adults
Do much to please others
And have therefore lost sight
Of the True Self.
This is the fullness of the ego's false self'.

The wise, know what makes them happy and sad,
But choose renunciation.
This is the end of the ego's false self'.

One Hundred and Fifty Five

In relation to a partner or a spouse
Do not speak of 'my' or 'mine'.
Do not think of 'his' or 'hers'

There is the possessor
And there is the possessed.
To be either
Is to be in a wrong relationship.

That which you own
Is not yours.
That which is owned
Does not belong.

In a true relationship
the two have become the one.

One Hundred and Fifty Six

In your relationship
With others
Be a mirror
That they may see
Their own goodness
Reflected in your own.
But never turn
The mirror on yourself.
This was the error
Of Narcissus.
he thought he saw
His own beauty
While all the time
Looking upon his own
Self-deception.

One Hundred and Fifty Seven

Fear is always selfish.
Compassion is
The executive arm of love.
Therefore do not be fearful
For the safety of others.
That is to regard your loss
As of more value than their suffering.
Express your concern for others
As compassion;
Suffering with them,
Not suffering because of them.

One Hundred and Fifty Eight

Choose to be imperfect.
What else can you do?
Imperfect in your understanding,
Imperfect in your relationships
Imperfect in your skills
Imperfect in your living.
None of it for adulation.
All of it for joy.
As long as you have joy in it,
You will not go far wrong.

One Hundred and Fifty Nine

Those are free
Who can choose.
Is obligation freedom?
Is fear?
Is duty freedom?
Is belief?
The ultimate freedom,
So a Sage says,
Is to be free about what to think.
Dare you be that free?

One Hundred and Sixty

Just as the image of the self
That evolves from the ego
Is a false self,
So the image of the One
That evolves from the ego
Is a false image.
It is the projection of fear
And desire.

The One has nothing
To define it but love.
When you encounter the One
You run out of words.

One Hundred and Sixty One

Boundaries are dangerous places.
Those who live without boundaries
Live without fear.
What is the difference
Between this and that,
Here and there?
Those who establish boundaries
Separate themselves
And create otherness.
Shall I let another person's opinions
Imprison me?
Shall I prevent access
To one who thinks differently
From me?
Love knows no boundaries.
Love sees no frontiers.

One Hundred and Sixty Two

The god we believe in
And the god we speak of
Is a figment of our imagination.
The god we experience
Is an altogether different matter.

One Hundred and Sixty Three

Light overcomes darkness.
Darkness cannot overcome light.

To overcome darkness
Light does nothing
But be itself.

Love overcomes evil.
Evil cannot overcome love.

To overcome evil
Love does nothing
But be itself.

One Hundred and Sixty Four

It is in the nature of birds to fly,
Yet young birds have to learn
To do what nature
Has equipped them for.

It is in the nature of men and women
To be spiritual
Yet they have to find a way
To experience their spirituality.

A Sage has said that
Humans are not physical beings
With souls;
They are spiritual beings
With bodies.

One Hundred and Sixty Five

Evidential faith
Is stronger than blind faith.
Blind faith accepts as evidence
Hearsay, face-value and feelings.
Evidential faith accepts
observation and experience.
If your beliefs are indefensible
Then they are also unreasonable.
Is it unreasonable to believe?

Faith is not belief in the unbelievable
But trust
in what can be observed
Of the Enabling.

One Hundred and Sixty Six

Finding fullness is as simple as breathing.
So is not finding it.

To discover the True Self
Abandon the ego's false self.

To remain a prisoner
Of the false Self,
Ignore the promptings
Of the True Self.

Everyone knows how to breath,
But few know how to live
In fullness.

One Hundred and Sixty Seven

Do not remark on kindness
As if it was the exception.
Make unkindness exceptional
With your disdain.

It is sad when the everyday
Becomes rare
And that which should be rare
Becomes the norm.

One Hundred and Sixty Eight

When people understand you
They think they have you in their power.
They may choose to listen
When it is to their advantage.
They may choose not to listen
If they think they understand
Your motives.

To the people
The wise are a mystery
And they deride them.
They are afraid because
They do not understand.
The wise understand
But will not say.

One Hundred and Sixty Nine

Those who are motivated
By the passions of the old brain
Are in darkness.

Those who are motivated
By the ingenuity of the new brain
Are in darkness.

Those who join
The passions of the old brain
With the ingenuity of the new brain.
Are in darkness.
This is the source of war.

Those who overcome
the passions of the old brain
With the ingenuity of the new brain
Are in darkness.
This is the source of religion.

The wise do not overcome,
They transcend.
Thus they realise
Everything enabled by the Self.

One Hundred and Seventy

The Sages said:
That which is most respected
Is most deeply hidden.
Thus, Truth cannot be known
Or understood,
In the way a riddle or sign
Is understood.
The wise experience it
As underlying all things.

When someone speaks,
The words may sound truthful
Though they are a lie.
Yet the wise recognise
The absence of truth,
Because they recognise
Its presence.

My Sages

The following are some of the most significant influences
that have brought this book into being.

Alan Watts
The Wisdom of Uncertainty

Bede Griffiths
A New Vision of Reality

Brian Swimme
The Universe is a Green Dragon

Carl Jung
Modern Man in Search of a Soul

Cyprian Smith
The Way of Paradox

Diarmuid O'Murchu
Reclaiming Spirituality

Eckhart Tolle
A New Earth

Ervin Laszlo
Science and the Akashic Field

Etty Hillesum
An Interrupted life

Jean Gebser
The Ever Present Origin

Joanna Macy
World as Lover, World as Self

John C.H. Wu
Tao Teh Ching

John O'Donohue
Anam Cara

Joseph Campbell
The Power of Myth
Hero with a Thousand Faces

Juan Mascaro
Upanishads
Bhagavad Gita

Karen Armstrong
The Battle for God

Ken Wilbur
Integrated Life Practice
(various authors)

Marcus Borg
The Meaning of Jesus

Norman Cohen
Cosmos, Chaos & the World to Come

Rabbi Lionel Blue
A Back Door to Heaven

Rumi
A Bridge to the Soul
Translated by Coleman Barks

Tim Ward
What the Buddha Never Taught

V.S. Ramachandran
Phantoms of the Mind

Maggie Ross
Silence: A User's Handbook

Laurens Van Der Post
Jung and the Story of our Times

Marija Gimbutas
The Goddesses and Gods of Old Europe

Peter Russell
From Science to God

Richard Rohr
True Self/False Self
(series on CD)
Immortal Diamond
Falling Upwards

Satish Kumar
You are Therefore I am

Thomas Merton
The Way of Chuang Tzu

Vinoba Bhave
Moved by Love

Robert Sardello
Silence: The Mystery of Wholeness

Rabindranath Tagore
The Songs of Kabir
Collected poems

Rassouli
Rumi Revealed

Swami Nikhilananda
The Gospel of Ramakrishna

Britain Yearly Meeting of Quakers
Quaker Faith and Practice

Beningus O'Rourke
Finding Your Hidden Treasure

Joel S. Goldsmith
The Thunder of Silence

About the Author
I had been involved with Christianity for over twenty years and during the latter ten my involvement was particularly intense. Then my faith evaporated. I left my Charismatic Christian church feeling disillusioned and bitter. During the next ten years I moved from disillusionment to neutrality to open-mindedness. Then I watched a TV series called 'The Power of Myth'. In it the comparative mythologist, Joseph Campbell, was interviewed by journalist Bill Moyers. Not exactly prime-time television but I was fascinated. Campbell explained the purpose of myth and I bought a transcript of the book.

Over the next twenty years I began to read many of the sources Campbell suggested and a lot more that suggested themselves. Primary to my reading were the Upanishads, the Bhagavad Gita and the Tao Te Ching. It gradually dawned on me that they threw new light on the Bible, which I had studied extensively during my fundamentalist Christian phase. During that phase I'd even attended courses in Koine Greek to better understand the New Testament. That background was not all loss because now my battered copy of the Bhagavad Gita is covered in pencilled references to passages in the Gospels and Epistles. Exposure to such a wide range of thinking helped me to recognise a common voice in all of it, a 'cantus firmus' that plays an underlying theme common to all religions. It revolutionised my own thinking and eventually my life.

In 2007, not having darkened the doorstep of any religious establishment for some 30 years, I attended a Quaker meeting. It had been recommended to me by a retired clergyman friend with whom I had been having some very interesting conversations about philosophy and religion. I was amazed to find a group of open minded people, many of whom had read the books I'd been reading and could understand and appreciate the spiritual ideas that had become so precious to me. I'd found a spiritual home. Nurtured and encouraged by my new friends, I began to write a book about my journey from fundamentalist Christianity to what I then regard as a real experience of faith. This exercise became a necessary deconstruction of my previous Christian beliefs and led to my becoming totally free of the need for doctrinally based belief.

In 2008 I began a journal. Over a long period of time I had experienced what James Joyce called 'epiphanies' (that which shines) and which the founder of the Quaker movement, George Fox, called 'Openings' – insights of a spiritual nature that helped me understand a little more about life and living it. Over the next four years my journal grew.

During that period I had two significant operations for cancer and began to feel that it might be a pity if some of what had been opened to me should be lost. So I set out to make a compilation of what I considered to be the most important entries. The problem I faced was that these were notes to myself, not something I'd ever envisaged publishing and, quite apart from my poor handwriting, they were too succinct and poorly expressed for others to gain much from them. Therefore I decided to rewrite the essence of them in the style of the early Taoist, Buddhist and Islamic sutras as they appear in English translations. This worked for me and the whole collection flowed out over a period of a few weeks. If you've read an English translation of the Tao Te Ching then some passages may seem to have been plagiarized. That is intentional but what I've always tried to do here is express my own experience of that ancient wisdom. Often a passage will be my own modern take on the thoughts written down by the Sages.

I'm at pains to emphasize that I don't see myself as a latter day Lau Tzu, neither do I have any knowledge of Taoism beyond that obtained from a few reliable translations of the Tao Te Ching. I'm not a theologian or a guru either, just an average sort of guy with a deep thirst for reality.

Printed in Great Britain
by Amazon